Gunner Gets $tocks

Written by: Charlesa Flatten

Published by Melanin Origins LLC
PO Box 122123; Arlington, TX 76012
All rights reserved, including the right of reproduction in whole
or in part in any form.
Copyright 2021

First Edition

The author asserts the moral right under the Copyright, Designs and Patents Act of 1988 to be identified as the author of this work.

This novel is a work of fiction. The names, characters and incidents portrayed in the work, other than those clearly in the public domain, are of the author's imagination and are not to be construed as real. Any resemblance to actual persons, living or dead, events or localities, is entirely coincidental.

All rights reserved. No part of this publication may be reproduced, stored in a retrieval system or transmitted, in any form by any means without the prior consent of the author, nor be otherwise circulated in any form of binding or cover other than that with which it is published and without a similar condition being imposed on the subsequent purchaser.

Library of Congress Control Number: 2021900684

ISBN: 978-1-62676-559-7 hardback
ISBN: 978-1-62676-558-0 paperback
ISBN: 978-1-62676-557-3 ebook

This book is dedicated to my two children who inspire me to be better each day. May you always do what makes you happy.

They took a trip to the bank, where they opened an investment account for Gunner and deposited his money.

Once home, Gunner asked his parents, "When can I buy stocks?" His dad smiled and asked Gunner, "What is a stock?"

Gunner answered, "Hmm... a stock something you buy so your money can make more money, right Mom?"

Gunner's face exploded with excitement as he asked, "How do I make money?"

Gunner responded, "Dividends? So I can keep the stock, let the price go up, and get paid just for keeping it." His dad replied, "Yes."

Gunner then asked, "How do I choose the right company to buy stocks from?"

Gunner's dad asked, "What's your favorite toy?" Immediately, Gunner ran out of the room, grabbed a monster truck, and handed it to his dad.

Excited to hear the great news, Gunner said, "I want to own a share of that company!" So, his mom bought Gunner a share of Flatten Toy Co.

Gunner put his hand on his chin as he looked around the room. He pointed at the computer and said, "I want to own a share of that company." His mom looked it up and said, "Good choice, G&H, Inc. also pays dividends." Then she bought Gunner a share of G&H Inc.

"Gunner", said Mom, "it looks like you have enough money for another share of Flatten Toy Co., or you can choose to invest in another company." Gunner took a moment to think about it, and, as he displayed a great, big smile he said, "Monster truck!" So, his mom bought another share of Flatten Toy Co.

"If the company continues to do well, you should see the amount of money in your account grow in time", said Dad.

Gunner's mom created stock certificates to display on his wall and said, "It is a really good idea to continue buying stocks. Dad and I will teach you more about investing as you grow in knowledge."

Later that evening, Gunner was admiring his stock certificates as his little sister came into his room. He showed them to her and said, "One day soon you will own stocks too."

About the Author

Charlesa Flatten is a Wife and Mom of 2. She served nearly a decade in the United States Navy and decided to transition after she became a mom. She enjoys spending time with her family, being in nature, dancing, and painting.

CPSIA information can be obtained
at www.ICGtesting.com
Printed in the USA
BVHW061323220421
605634BV00013B/1545